Songs for the Band Unformed

John Passant

Songs for the Band Unformed

Songs for the Band Unformed
ISBN 978 1 76041 194 7
Copyright © text John Passant 2016
Cover image: Daniel Spellman

First published 2016 by
GINNINDERRA PRESS
PO Box 3461 Port Adelaide 5015 Australia
www.ginninderrapress.com.au

Contents

Introduction	7
Our bombs are love	9
In the land of never	10
We are the one	12
I will be shopping, today	15
Long to rain over us	16
Take my hand	19
Will you walk with me?	21
I looked into your eyes	22
There is no other way – the 3.23 a.m. version	23
Impromptu: can I stand and poet?	25
This is for you	26
The carcass of caress	29
The legs of happiness are closed	30
Will no one sing my songs?	31
The morning is come	32
We must not fail	34
And the sun fights back, again	38
Chanting yesterday's truths at tomorrow	39
Welcome barbed wire world	40
We are gone, all gone	41
I saw you at the mall	43
Veranda storm	44
The grim within	45
Here comes the hearse	46
I can hear the violins	48
And I shall wear my scarf again	49
I shall go	51
I do not write any more	53
Old poets dream and gather	54

I shall walk to the beach	55
Whose dead are these?	56
We are, our land	57
There is no other way	59
There are no poets any more	61
I can write no more tonight	62
Let there be no mourning	63
To vote, perchance to dream	64
The prison that sets us free	65
The sea is calm tonight	66
The flatline poetry	68
For sleep the enemy to win	69
The slow lane of history	70
Oh, we can't tax the rich	72
The returning son	74
Only catching love to play	75
I had a poem last night	76
Poets are not generals	77
The hope of the despairing	78
The dark days of light	79
Unknown joy	81
The joy of Wollongong	82
Daylight saving again	83

Introduction

When I was sixteen, I told the careers adviser who had come to my school that I wanted to be a poet. He was flummoxed. In the twenty-five years of giving such advice, I was the first person to ever say that to him. He suggested I look for something – anything – that might be more conventional and more monetarily sustaining.

Instead of writing poetry, I chose to study law and economics at university to give me the wherewithal to change the world. It was, after all, the late 60s and early 70s, a time of great upheaval and radicalisation. Oh, sweet naivety of youth!

After a lifetime in tax, including as a tax academic and then as a senior officer in the Australian Tax Office, I 'retired' in 2008 and began writing again. This involved left-wing and socialist political analysis on my blog En Passant and, more recently, writing for progressive online media outlet Independent Australia. But poetry kept erupting irregularly and episodically.

In between various jobs, including a return to a much diminished tax academy for what was unfortunately a short time, at sixty-one I decided I wanted to publish some of the poems I had written in the six years since my retirement. In part, this was to see if my work went beyond doggerel. In part, it was to feed the ego. In part, it was, as I had done for many students, to inspire others.

This volume of poems is the result. They are a mix of the personal and the political. As well as tax, the liberation of humanity by the mass of ordinary working people has been a key element in my intellectual development and understanding of the world. Some of that I hope shows through in some of the poems.

Taxing the rich is one of the more clearly recognisable possible songs in the collection. (As an aside, if there are any bands out there who want to put one or more of my poems to music – a double poetry, in my view – then please contact me.)

The usual terrors of love and desire, of self-doubt, of longing, and of joy and happiness, find expression here. So too does my horror with much of the world today, with its barbarity, its wars, its monetary and spiritual poverty, and its cruelty.

However, there is hope. Like Gramsci, I have a pessimism of the intellect and an optimism of the will. Like Trotsky, I rejoice that life is beautiful. Like him, I believe that future generations will cleanse it of all evil, oppression and violence, and enjoy it to the full.

If a reader says 'Yes, I understand' or, even better, 'Yes, I feel', then my labours have not been in vain. To those readers, then let me say – enjoy, understand and, most importantly, feel.

There are many people to thank, including my children Michael and Louise, and my father, Joe. However, there is one person I owe my life and my love to, and that is Patricia. Thank you for everything: for your support, your care and gentleness, and most of all for your love.

Patricia, I dedicate this book with love to you.

John Passant
August 2016

Our bombs are love

Our bombs are the bombs of your freedom
Raining down our reign
On all, the children, women, men,
We can
Enjoy our freedom in your grave
With your missing body parts
This is our art

Their bombs are the enemy of freedom
Raining hate upon your land
Sowing cemeteries so you understand
The difference in the dead and maimed

Our bombs are love
Theirs are not
Remember that as you hold
Your children to your heart
Dead in our noble cause
Dead in our noble wars

And remind yourself
We are the liberators
Embrace us too
Our killing is for you

This is a cause for joy
Grieve not your girl, or boy
Nor anger your response
Except against the enemy
For soon, very soon
We will set you free

In the land of never

It is the wakefulness that walks its want
In the middle of our night
It is the darkness that haunts the space
Between despair, and delight
Where stands the man
Whose hand is caught, alight
And the woman who wakes alone
Screaming our words of fright
And gathers the older one
For whom the sun is gone
Knowing the dawn is come
To challenge all our songs
The words might echo long
Upon the past that is
The tune however bides it time
And questions all that is
For nothing exists beyond
The limits of the living
Where children hug their shadows
In the land of the unforgiving
And run free among amok
To places that do not stop
And clock the time that will not rhyme
With sidelines of the cheering
Return to beds alive with minds
And the sleep that is the thinking
Arising anew unrenewed
Into the world of blinking
Eyeing the past into the future
Bound, found, unground

Floating again, away again
That, my friend, is our end
All morphed away and here to stay
In her arms awake to all
And sleeping there forever
This is the aim, this is the call
In the land of never.

We are the one

As a boy I rowed
The river of religion
Now I have forgiven
My torment
As a man I sail
Socialism's seas
And its storms
Encalm me
Now the confluence
Flows backward
And the two begin anew
One, social justice,
Rusts us to nirvana
Leaving the other, alone
There is no home
For halfway houses of reform
That crawl past
Slow, not fast
To nowhere but behind
The cross of loss
Is not mine
But ours
We have the power
To change their world
We stay in bed
Blanket headed
Until, until
That is the question
When, upon reflection,
Our gods are gone

That is the answer
Not just the gods above
But those we love, here and now
The secular love of saviours
Such strange behaviours
Lead us to the abyss
A papal kiss
Will not save us
Nor the old ways
Grace us
I pray for your loss
Which is the winning
We are a broad church
Of one eyed men
And women too
But this you knew
Did you understand?
Is this your land?
Or just mining postponed till
The night falls?
Where are the calls
That resonate, for justice?
Too late and left behind
All in my mind
There are no confessions
Only lessons from the past
Let us raise our glass
To what will come
I am not the one
You are not the one

There are no gods
On heaven and on earth
To give birth
To the new
Needs us all
We are the one
This you will know
One day
One day

I will be shopping, today

I will be shopping, today
For tofu and toilet paper
And, in a way,
Sugar that isn't
These are the daily steps
This man takes
Of shopping, and washing
And reading of our wakes
Then writing the blog
That no one reads
Expressing their hopes
or fulfilling my needs?
Where Facebook takes hold
And ages us, growing old
We become the past
And only last
In bitter words
These are the ways,
Every day,
Of walking the dog
And learning, to stay
Waiting for postwomen and letters
Knowing that change
Is never mailed
Have I failed?
Not at all
That is my call
And so I return
I have done the shopping today

Long to rain over us

We live in a world
of their bombs

Where the armed panopticon
eyes us all
kills the small
the poor,
the fallen

What for? the prophet asks
There are no tasks
but profit
All profit

Cower before its power
At the altar of the last
Remember no past
And gather guns
that run the mind
of time

There is no wine
to drink away
Today, or tomorrow
Our worry, their sorrow

The bombs reign
While drones dominate
We are too late

There is no refuge
From this hate
And so we start

The past, past heart
is caught between
love and the fate
that awaits
the limbs, separated
the people, berated

Stand silent
Slaughter untold
Unfolds, violent
not quiet, not quite
alone, above

There is no love
Only bombs
the weapons of aplomb

Our power
is the hour
of their death
nothing left
But the fleeing
of the seeing

They knew
On death row
No life allowed
Only money, hallowed

And so ends
their eyeless walk
their tongueless talk
Their eyeless gaze
all of us, raised
to the ground

All found
All lost
There is no cost
But our lives

Their lives count
And challenge not bombs
But humanity

They are bombed
We remain, unfree

Take my hand

I cannot take your hand
Boy in the sand and surf
I cannot take your hand
And bring you to my earth

Power had the chance,
And did nothing but its dance
To the song of race
Know your place they yelled

Their helled shouts rise below
The waves that hold humanity
We all flee
The bombed city

Where the civilised
Rain freedom
Dressed in death
Nothing is left

But the dead
Upon our shores
Where walk the whores of power
Now is the hour

To rise, rise against
Their armies, of defence,
And the order that destroys
Children and their toys

And you and me
Our cause is free, to be,
The freedom you now have
We cannot grant to them

Our wishes
Cannot breath your kisses
Take my hand, here is my land
The casket of your dreams

Will you walk with me?

Will you walk with me
Through the gentle hello
Where quiet duvet
Meets screamed pillow

Where the sun of evil
Wrestles the night of calm
And lock-stepped presence
Oils its balm?

Where the battles that challenge
The rattles within
Portend no end
Only next of kin

And the rising each day
Gives its way
To the penalty rates
That are life's astray

Then will you walk with me
Through the gentle goodbye
Always questioning,
Never asking why?

I looked into your eyes

I looked into your eyes
The other day
Perhaps for the first time
In all those years
Since I caressed your wine
I have not remembered
Your soul
Not been able to
Or your laugh
A sad laugh
The other day
Nervous, in a way
Like your talking
You were mourning
Life given, life torn
Mother taken
Borne aloft
This is the cost
Of life
I looked into your eyes
The other day
Was it for
The last time?

There is no other way – the 3.23 a.m. version

I have woken to the days of little time
Where blackness stretches back
And no birds are singing sweet upon the line
The crawling creatures of the night attack
And undermine the lack, the lack of mind

There is no other way to stay
The stillness that arrays the time
All in our mind and place to find
The piece that is the peace
The rest that is the sleep

And all to keep the agony alive
Where changes second hand
Are driven slow and fast
This cannot, must not, last
It does

Until the horn sounds blast
Growing ever growing
Coming ever coming, fast
Life is the numbing in between
Where we walk, unseen

And play our role
Here is the scene,
There is its toll
Where the great gather
Drowning dreams

All is not, as it seems
The light catches our moment
And the seamstress stitches
Dreams of witches haunt the woken
It suits, bespoken

And the word is taken
Not heard
For there is no ear
That catches fear
Like the memory of tomorrow

Where hangs the fallen fruit
Is that it?
Is that the root?
Or just the taking of today
There is no other way.

Impromptu: can I stand and poet?

I can stand
And talk
I can stand
And walk
I can even stand
And recite

These are not the same
As poetry
On the night
Is there art involved?
Or the porn of words?
A place of joy
Or a factory of turds?

Made up,
On the spot
God she is good
Damn he is not

Do I have a place?
Dare I save my face?
For later
Always later

Come forth, self-hater
And sing a poem now
For you know how
You know how

This is for you

The retreat beckons
With meaning or without
A reckoning arrives
My friend, the doubt

Late again, it survives
and runs its hands
To my out side
Nowhere to hide
Not even here
All is fear, all is drear
All is gone, again

The pain of nothing
Where existing is
Forbearance,
Love is clearance
For nothing is clear
Did you not hear?

The aid no longer works
The cane is thrashing
Hips are lashing knees
Is life my tease?
Or the place of please
And thank you?

Where thank resembles
A Germanic-rooted word
A rooted world,
of yes sir no sir
No one to care

My, your hair is grey
Why do you ask?
There is no other way
There is no other task

Exiting is forbearance too
But of course
That is what you knew,
Is it not?
This must stop

But only when the last
Slave ship
upends itself
On the reefs of justice
Can the end be upped,
And justice supped

And the rule
That is the tyranny of one,
Inside
Felt, too deep,
Hide, asleep

The arctic melt of help
Too far away, gone today
Never to refreeze
That is the end of ease

We march our way,
An army of alone
Casting days into stone

The headstones
Of the past
Do not last
Their flesh bleeds
In the rain
And the wind and storm
Of life,
Seeds, remains

The sunshine too erodes,
Corrodes,
Solid air
Who cares?

I do, but in the caring
Lose the caring
In the sharing
Lose the sharing
And in the daring
Lose the do

This is for you

The carcass of caress

There is no doubt but the doubt
There is no way but the out

With these words we comfort blindness
Caught in the talons of their kindness
And challenge nothing but the see
To quash the yearning, to be free

To be free, aye there's a rub
A young child, a crying bub
Who lies alone, all alone
A persona, loud, unknown

For hangs the carcass of caress
In the stages of our undress
While all the bonds are broken here
The children sing, the fear is near

The old young man limps to home
Scarred, war weary, through his bones
No light in houses of the street
No people welcome or to meet

Do not, do not, again
End that way, my refrain
But take the gutter from its hole
And dig the life that swallows whole

The soul we used to have but gone
All apace and all sweet wrong
For there is no doubt but the doubt
There is no way but the out

The legs of happiness are closed

The gunnels are gone,
The legs of happiness closed
All is wrong
Except for those
Who drone and bomb
And kill
The children still,
Remain
Still,
While the kings of freedom
Spread their peace
In the coffins, lying,
Uncreased, the young
The old
The pensioners of streets
No meat
They eat the promises
Of politicians, not left
Bereft
There is no other way
The bankers' theft will stay
Today, tomorrow
This is not sorrow
But despair
Who cares?
The legs of happiness are closed

Will no one sing my songs?

Will no one sing my songs
Take my words
and belong,
Own the life of them
Revive their dead
And survive this old man
Another day?
Go, play.

The morning is come

I have been to the land
Where men do not cry
No one asks why
I have been to the waters
Where women weep
No one sleeps

While winter wiles
Lies smile
And the cold
Clasps our hands
In grand designs

Where wisdom wines,
This place drinks,
Lacks the thoughts,
And thinks
Of noughts
And breaking brinks
That turn the tumbril through
What to do?

These are the words
That rebound
Never lost, always found
No need to search

Our truth alerts
And what for?
Here walks the door
That holds the clue
Nothing left,
At least for you

And for me remains
The gains, decline
While the sun arrives
The frost dissolves
And solves? Nothing.

A wet lawn
Still, forlorn,
Beckons beyond
All done
All gone

The morning is come
Nowhere to run
But within, the marathon
Springs anew
For me, and you

We must not fail

I have searched the other side
I have nothing to hide
But is there one?
Taking fun from all
A fun that only guns can stop
That is the sop
To freedom

I have searched our side
What are we left with
Or without?
The hordes of no doubt
Bowing before false gods
That have truth
In their nods and kneels
This is how it feels

No more, here is the door
'We'll give you what for'
And bounce me out
To cheers, no doubt,
What louts to carry us
Forward in the last place
At a hastening pace

Never slowly, at full bore
There is no more
To do or not to do
There is no question
Only a lectern
Of hate, it is too late
To change, for love

Is that our role?
To be the love
That hate stole?
And bury that enemy, within,
The whole place grim for happiness
With one caress
That ends the beginning

Or ends, the beginning
My hair is not thinning
But my gut is
I lie, and lie and lie
Awake, alone,
There is no phone
To talk to anyone

That is the fun
Taken and twisted
Laughter lifted
From the back of the bus
Let's make a fuss
And no one notices
No one responds

The Daily Ageing
grows on and on
For too long
Our unity is built strong
On sands of order
Reigning in Berlin
Can we begin

Or shall we be
Sisyphus falling back
Rolling, rolling, rolling
Past the past?
It cannot last
But does, driven down
From above

I plant the seeds
And everywhere grow
The weeds of yesterday
It is too slow
For me or mine
'Relax and drink the wine'
It will do, and does

Is there no more
To ask, ask, ask,
To fail our task
Or in the building,
Reflect?
Just another reject
On the road to nowhere

Who cares?
The time demands we do
The future demands we must
In you I trust
There will be our lifetime
A place, a time of love
Will prevail

We will grow, I tell myself,
That is the point of this tale
And risings past and present
Not to resent but to love,
We may be frail,
But for our future
We must not, cannot fail.

And the sun fights back, again

The cold wind chases sun away
At the tea-chaied seaside
Where the children play
While parents and friends unsay
The world as is

The laughter of the kids
Echoes the waves,
Rolling on, and on, not caring
But the boardies do,
Sharing surf and nature

As the sun fights back,
I attack my past
Through café glass
It cannot last

This coast, this coast,
Of walks and talks and people
Where emotions cascade,
And steeple, on parade,
The foetal man becomes the boy
That is a joy

But now the sun is gone
The surfers pub along
While, silent to us now,
The waves roll on, and on
For tomorrow, always tomorrow
Where our happiness is hollow
Until today liberates our way
And the sun fights back, again

Chanting yesterday's truths at tomorrow

All the poets are dead
Buried in the old well

All the singers are mute
Living the hell of others' sound

All the musicians are quiet
Crawling underground

All the painters are panicked
With no colours found

There is no room for them
In a world of men
And women
Chanting yesterday's truths at tomorrow

Welcome barbed wire world

Welcome barbed wire world
Not golden curled
But unwatered, unfed
It is here they bled
The outsider, no within
We are the kin
Of all
While we fall,
Died of lies
Recalls the past
The future folds
Not told
But written
In your hand
Become our land
When you flee
You are me
Where hope is us,
In disgust
All quiet, all torn
A terrible beauty, forlorn
Our land,
Whose hand rejects
And claims right ridden
To eject
Kids, wives, mothers
Of no crime,
It will be your time
It is your time

We are gone, all gone

There is no rain in my land
Where fires, the imagination, is real
And where the bonfire
The deniers deserve,
Is served, platter plated, to the poor
Drowning in air-conditioned comfort
That flames, encouraged by the same, tame,
And then destroy

There is no joy in my land
Only the politics out of hand
And half-rigged boats that gloat
As they sink beneath the ocean's float
To scream, where is my dream?

It is over there, the land of rain become,
Another place, another run
Of profits and their prophets
Seeing nothing, knowing all
Before the fall

We are all
Before the fall

Another tree, another house
That was a home
All alone, we watch,
We see,
Nature's man-made victory

There is no land in my land
Only gold, panned, burnished, burnt,
Remains in the ruins of Absalom
We are gone, all gone

I saw you at the mall

I saw you at the mall
Pretending not to notice
Did you forget those times
Of hurried kisses, and more,
Before the serious summer challenged me?

Just me, not you,
Your time was pleasure
Mine was love, and passion
The joining threatened, threatened
To combine the two
That you knew

And so I fled,
We have not spoken
Except in my dreams,
My desires,
Where I scream
Relight those fires

It will not be,
The glaciers of love
Have avalanched that past
But the memories, the memories last

I saw you at the mall
You did not notice

Veranda storm

From my veranda
I can see the storm, coming,
Sometimes close, sometimes far,
Rolling over mangy mountains
Never breaking, but threatening,
Threatening all the time,
I hear its rhyme,
An echo from another place,
Another age,
When rains raged against the buildings of the old
Until the dreams crashed, and the cold set in
What do we do now?
We begin, we begin.

The grim within

There is a grim within that gathers and grows
And catches the grass in its throes
It flames the ground to its belows
And wells the land of our sorrow
The fire's end is all we know
The phoenix rising has burst the snow
And the grim within gathers again
And the grim within grows its pain

Here comes the hearse

There is no sound
Just the silence of the rain
And the fighting within
That begins, again and again
To bury the future
In our pain

The handshake yesterday
Will repay emotion, now
Wrought thought riddled
Past the talk
Of commotion, not quiet
But rioting, outside

What will it bring
Inside? Nothing,
We hide, aside,
in the open
The enemy can see
It is me

And your talk
walks past
This cannot last
Not in the time we have
For better or for worse
Here comes the hearse

And so ends, this chapter
Caught in laughter
Hereafter known
As I, the one alone,
Too alone
Without you

I can hear the violins

I hear Trotsky sing
And march, violin in hand
Trudge, trudge trudging,
Parched,
Through our red, black, ancient land

The song, the band, the poetry,
Cascade and echo down
The winding paths
That are history

Our words, renowned, set free,
Fire other places
There are even glimpses of our faces
Before their gattled guns quiet
Other riots of gentle folk
This is not a joke

The violins continue
In lands away, askew
Returning to their homes
In music writ anew
On bones the same, replayed, replayed

And once again the song begins
Of Sisyphus in a land of kings
We start the climb
For their peak to win
And I can hear the violins,
I can hear the violins

And I shall wear my scarf again

The wine glass, shattered, stands,
broken, in my lonely hand
A cry for people
Without land

No one cares
About Palestine
No one cares
He sips his wine

Long gone, and beyond
Vision early, taken late
Who can wait?
Not Gazans, at their gate

The wall of hate
Constructed on the lies
Who dies?
The children, our children, die

Without a by-your-leave
Or why
They leave, the children
For their sky

And I will wear my scarf again
To keep the cold from entering
And bay the worlds of hate,
Is it all too late, too late?

Maybe not,
By what resistance shows
Support grows
And scarves and broken wine glasses portend
An end, a happy end?

I shall go

I do not ride any more
Not now,
Not even before
But past today becomes
The present ever numb

And in the style unknown
Where children, overgrown,
Live full their lives
Of futility
What can it be?

A lovers' tiff, perhaps,
That gathers pace,
What if we run
To another place?

It can be
Our friend, our enemy
A quiet Western Front
It chooses you, and me

All quiet, our wants
All quiet, our desires
All quiet all
On burning pyres
Of tortured times

Who has the time
Not I
That is why,
Why, what?
What have you got?

I do not know
I do not know
I shall go
Yes, I shall go

I do not write any more

The words do not read any more
And the books look on, unlooked
While I am caught
A taut teacher of the past
Where time tastes sweet
But does no last

For in the beginning
Was the word,
Absurd, we cry,
We do not ask why

There is much more
Written in the place
Where the sword is mighty
and the pen, the pen is what?

A blot, a failure
A time of rot
And rottenness
I will confess
I do not write
I bless

Old poets dream and gather

I remember
Your body in December
Was my summer,
Of content, oh what content!

Our fleeting thoughts, entwined,
Made whole, unwound,
Rejoined, unbound
And that was it,
unbound, unfound

It must have been the times
Chained to change
Its need greater than me
No smashing the chains now

Could we return to December,
Do you remember, unshackled,
Where time bent is spent
on memories of now
And how we are

We are? What?

Old poets dream and gather
the present from our past
It is the last, not ours
But moments joined of each
Within our reach then, and now?

I shall walk to the beach

I shall walk to the beach
With the sun before me
And an old man beside me
Past yesterday's coffee shops
And tawdry trees of better days
Where young women in bikinis
Spark memories of waves and riding
Where sand clasps the toes
Screaming do not go
And salt invades the nose
Weighing heavy as the sea invites us in
It's almost 'where you bin?'

I have been away
Too long, too far, too tired
Every day recycled, some might say retired
But now the son returns
And shining, burns old ways,
The walks, the plays
And the never ending waves, always waves
Pounding and drowning, calming and snaking
Into the memory, again,
There is no pain but joy
I am returned, I am a boy.

Whose dead are these?

It is the hope of the despairing
Not caught but wearing
Life in vests
Escaping the empty nest
Taken, not blessed,

Upon the sea, the holy sea
Of cant and won't be
In our place,
Belonging is their other face
Staring, staring, staring
Upon our shores

Whose dead are these? The question asks
And the answer crashes on our masks
Yours; they are yours

We are, our land

This is the day of no days
The time of the end
Where the past
Does fend for ways
To bury the past

Among the graves are grown
Men and women known to none
Unknown, alone
Buried in the cloak of history
But not for me

Children's stolen days apologise
For presence, in our eyes,
The white picket fence
Never lies, but grows
The mining hoes

Here is a warrior
The she that cannot be
Herself, no one else
Her blood cries the soil
For all, the toil

And the fail, safe behind the land
not planned, not rights
There are no nights
In a land without sun
And a son without land

Hear then this demand
White man in the big house
Of cattled coal and wheat
We are, our land
This is not defeat

There is no other way

I am old
Not wizened in the ways
Of turpentine trays
And analytic days

Where paint is a past time
And thinking
A game of rhyme
For the old man singing in C
What is there but to be?

Vegies live too
Do they sprout for you?
Or dragged out, survive?
Is this alive?

The slow steady humdrum
Of fiery tedium
Means we strive strive strive,
For their medium
And having reached the best,
Average the less, away

There is no other than the shoe worn walk
To the place that talks
of work and other things
We see the rings that others hear

And in our fear
Remove the eyes of yesterday
There is no other,
There is no other way

They have banished the poets
To the land where actions rule
And all the time they question
Who needs a silly old fool?

No one screams the answer
And takes their place at dinner
Where talk is of politics
My, how you're getting thinner!

While the head is fattened
On their warmed over diet
I have read the poet's book
And maybe you should try it

There are no poets any more

There are no poets
Any more
Only plaintiffs
Searching for the sure

In our sea, uncertainty,
Why wait for more?
The saintly Tom thumbs
His bum so respectfully

And words, strung out
Like heroines in doubt,
Shout, to the heavens
Leave us unleavened

And we do, nothing rising
Nor baked in thought, surprising
That captures the soul
Until the part becomes the whole

Fragments, all apart
Not joined, not hearts
In love but separated
From above

To join, that is the how
The words scan nought
For you and me
The end is fought
There is no now

I can write no more tonight

I can write no more
Tonight
The rage is gone
A light, is dying gentle

And the words, broken,
Are eaten, alive
Where is the token, sense,
Beating back sweet chants of innocence?

All gone, there is no more
A deserted desert for a floor
With roofs ahead,
And blackened bars the door

The distance gallops all awry
For what else is there
But the cry
And the answer, we know,
But why?

Not here, not now
Then when?
And in the coming of the past
The knowing is the pen

But time is fast
Where age forgone
Is age foretold
Still, wrong and old

I can write no more
Tonight

Let there be no mourning

Let there be no mourning
When tomorrows become today
In that space where the dawning
Blasts the grasping past away

The tired tears the fears display
It is another morning
It is another day

And we wake not taken
But alive again
To fight, my friend
To the end, to the end.

To vote, perchance to dream

To vote, perchance to dream; aye, there's the rub,
For in that vote of death, what dreams may come,
When we have shuffled off this electoral coil,
Must give us pause.

The prison that sets us free

Too many times I have walked
With the wobbly boot strapped firmly on
And seen the family of the mourn
Sing to the tune of a rising sun

There is no toast as fake friends embrace
And their witty banter takes another face
Being drunk to heroes from the long ago
While we brain addled plead, we did not know

The times are closed, too early it seems
The pouring rains upon our dreams
The laughter ebbs as the drinking drains
Another glass to fuel our brains

We solve the future in table talk
Where many run we can but walk
For outside lurks new reality
The prison that sets us free

The sea is calm tonight

The sea is calm, tonight
And the waves of anger, tight,
Have bought a peace
And still the silence grows
That no one knows

Close and yet afar
We talk, ajar
While our words
Upon the water fall
Lost to me, lost to all

Cascading chasms of the quiet
Unite their purpose
In our riot
And so we stand,
Victims of your promised land

The cell of freedom beckons
In this or other lives
We reckon on our own
Not counting their hard blown
But challenging, alone, always alone

We hear the music near
While the siren sings
To queer the pitch and yawl
There is no other,
Only all, only all

This island that is us
Is born of lies
Amid our trust disguised
Nowhere to go
Nowhere to hide

The sea is calm, tonight.

The flatline poetry

The darkness embraces and enfolds
Like a jumper growing old
Warm and comfortable
But in the wearing ends
Its warmth and comfort
And the friends are cold
With buttonholes of discontent

The wake and mourning every morning
The take and fawning every day
These stitch our cloth cut deep
From misery, asleep
And raise the hand, timid,
To ask the question why
And in the reaching
Touch their sky
To feel the moment free
And so end the flatline, poetry
End the flatline poetry.

For sleep the enemy to win

And if I do not sleep
There is no sound
But feeling free
Lies unbound

While your night crawls
And catches all
Except the eye
That is my I

Where to now
The question's sprung
The dawning rise,
The rising sun?

Or images of walk
That fade within
The half heard talk
And gather, gather to the end

With tethered lather
Be my friend
For all is gone
But your handed tend

Your handed tend
That led
And stroked me
To my bed

For sleep the enemy to win

For sleep the enemy to win

The slow lane of history

There is no return
But the road and its wend
That takes our way to an end

Not hand in hand
But grappled, friend
To a journeyman of bitter, lemon,
The fruit that hints of heaven
And rises, unleavened, to its hell

Who can tell, who can tell?

That is the question
Of the quest,
And for the rest
They line the street
To greet the walkers
Not with hellos
But blows of claps

Poor chaps, and women
Must fend alone, together
And hunt in packs of individuals
Made hole by work

And whole by working,
The jerking payday of slavery,
Like a key
Unlocks our future
A twist and are we free?

This is what I see
As the first steps taken
Lead to a martini world, shaken
And stirred

What better word to describe the life
More active than the past
With the future rushing fast
In the slow lane?

The slow lane, of history,
Is what I see
Is what I see.

Oh, we can't tax the rich

Oh, we can't tax the rich
Cause they make all the jobs
And we can't tax the rich
'Cause they are f…g nobs

If we tax the rich
They'll depart our fine shores
If we tax the rich
They'll avoid our tax laws

So let's not tax the rich
And make this place their heaven
Let's not tax the rich
Just like in *Ocean's Eleven*

So shovel all our money
To Gina and the gang
Force it down their gullets
And go out with a bang

The richer Murdoch is
The better off we will be
So join in the choir
And sing along with me

No tax, no tax, no tax
Except for you and me
No tax, no tax, no tax,
That will set them free

No tax, no tax, no tax
Except for you and me
No tax, no tax, no tax,
There lies our poverty

So if you want good schools
And hospitals as well
And decent pensions too
Send the rich to hell

Let's tax the rich instead
And hear them cry no more
Let's tax the rich instead
Until there are no poor

I imagine this little ditty being sung by a strong-voiced woman strumming a steel guitar. Or maybe a punk band going crazy.

The returning son

The guitar gifted one
Who slings his arrows as the son
Departs, town gone, for too long
With the tumbrils rumbling past history's door
To take a moment and to floor
The yesterday that lives in awe
Of nothing

And breaking chains, we rearrange
The furniture of future days
In lounges of the living
Still, forgiving, quiet and believing
For we are leaving
And the journey's end has just begun
To take us to the returning son,
The returning son

Only catching love to play

There is a gaining in the loss
That brings together hope and fear
And blends the meaning of our words
To the passage of the year
As the silence on the streets
Echoes down the path of tears
And captures all our trodden times
In the birthplace of our wares
Will you walk again this way?
Or pass another's place to stay
Where there are no others resting
Only catching love to play
Only catching love to play

I had a poem last night

I had a poem last night
Of fright and fear and fancy
But sleep has robbed the words
And the patterns that,
Absurd,
Had passed for insight,
Are gone,
To delight no one
And fall among the dreams
Caught between the streams
Of the waking and the dead
All read, but only read,
In that space, my turning head
And pass away
Like shadows of the day
As the night descends, to the end

Poets are not generals

Poets are not generals
tramp, tramp, trampling,
to the tune of the dead,
the people's revolution, its head
smashed against reaction's rock

Yet rising to mock and batter down
the ratted gown of despots
with their plans and plots

That is not us, we cry
and die under their bullets
and take Christ's cue,
to begin anew
the task of freedom's mask
lifted from its twisting chains,
caught in the rhyme of rain to bear the fruit

And let the time, so dissolute, dissolve

We poets are not generals
in the theatres of their war,
the bosses' whore,
but saviours of the spark
that leads us from their dark
and inspires worlds
that twirl and whirl sweet freedom's space
behind our face, impassive and inert,
until the grin of winning takes its place
and we stand among the trees, free,
reading, not bleeding.

The hope of the despairing

It is the hope of the despairing
Not caught but wearing
Life in vests
Escaping the empty nest
Taken, not blessed,
Upon the sea, the holy sea
Of cant and won't be in our place
Belonging is their other face
Staring, staring, staring
Upon our shores
Whose dead are these? The question asks
And the answer crashes on our masks
Yours; they are yours

The dark days of light

Three degrees, sparse, stark, bare
Caught beyond the watered where
Glance fevered, fervid fools
Blanche tethered, turgid tools
And the silent scream
Dreams the universe
Is gathered, worse,
Is revenged, avenging abuse
To what use?
Of theirs no doubt
And the clout
Of dictators' gold
Grown old in vaults, foretold
In books that make no sense
And called hence from after life
To live with fire, always fire
The burns are rife,
On the pyre, to profit right
That is the point, to profit right
Their smokey joint, plumes away
Brings us joy, dark lights of day
The joy of struggle, wages fight
And sleep for years between
Not covered, never seen
Until the pain forces, but forces what?

I am not, I am not
But they are now, and how,
While the plains pain plenty in their plough
And the birds sing tears
From our yesteryears
Silent in their chorus
For them, not us
We are beyond their quiet
And caught in the dance
The slow, twirling dance
Of withered weather
Where no chance, taken
Upon those forsaken
And left rotting, all rotting
For everywhere
Are the dark days of light
The dark days of light.

Unknown joy

There is a joy
we will never know
written fast, taken slow
And gathered ground
around
to take the place
where life is face
in others' eyes
and strip disguise
from Christian reticence
Not caught but taught
defence, always the fence
who slips the knot away
and sails for today
A town where time is you
calls to play, to do
And then disappears
like wide clip shears
But gone is the gathered
And gathered is the gone
Done wrong for heaven
To the hell of the way
Do not stay
Go, go away.

The joy of Wollongong

What beauty, father heart in tow,
To walk the beach, and sit aglow,
Sun taken, not forsaken,
Waved bodies sculpting sand,
And to drift, beyond the man,
To nature's rendered hand,
Such is the joy of Wollongong.

Daylight saving again

The sun is come
and the shadows fall
like statues of John Howard

The walk is run
and the clocks are set
to fast forward for an hour

October is the cruelling month
of revolution and credit, crunch

Where roos a'bound
through grass so brown
with the hound upon the hunt

Nothing caught but breath, and stableness
abandoned in the fury

The cows and goat greet every bloat
with belch and fart and duty

And as we talk, this dog and I
the time returns and the future cries

It is the past but full of lies

And the savage one then
begs his only question

Can we last in this direction?

The sun is gone
there is no mention
of the fast
or the forward

We trudge back from our beginning
and see the ghost of Howard,
grinning

The bark is whimpered and we go
inside cowed

www.ingramcontent.com/pod-product-compliance
Lightning Source LLC
Chambersburg PA
CBHW062145100526
44589CB00014B/1690